I MET GOD TODAY

Ordinary Events Seen with New Eyes

Danny Brock, General Editor

Reflections written by the students of Saint Andrew's
Regional High School, Victoria, Canada

Saint Mary's Press®

The reflections in this book were written over several years by eighth-grade students attending Saint Andrew's Regional High School in Victoria, Canada.

The reflections were collected and collated by their teacher, Mr. Danny Brock. Brock is a religious educator and retreat director and author of *Teaching Teens Religion* and *Catholicity Ain't What It Used to Be* (dcbrock.com).

The art in this book was created by four students from Saint Andrew's Regional High School and Pacific Christian School: Alexandrea Delos Reyes, Paula Cota, Gloria Wong, and Chanel Mandap.

The content in this resource was acquired, developed, and reviewed by the content engagement team at Saint Mary's Press. Content design and manufacturing were coordinated by the passionate team of creatives at Saint Mary's Press.

Cover images from Shutterstock.

Printed in the United States of America

5043

ISBN 978-1-59982-918-0

Contents

Introduction

Eighth graders are a delight to teach. I teach them Religion.

Eighth-grade students have one foot in elementary school and one foot in high school. They are the best of both worlds. They are not "middle" anything.

Fresh, open, and uninhibited like little kids, yet equipped with a new ability to think metaphorically, allegorically, and analogically. Their spirit hovers between childhood and adolescence, giving them a rare view of both. It is a view worth noting.

I'll admit I wasn't expecting too much when I first announced my Religion assignment.

"I want you to write a booklet of stories entitled *I Met God Today*."

They looked at me.

"This will be the hardest assignment I will give you this year," I said.

They agreed.

I had done my best, over the preceding weeks, to prepare them. I had shown the claymation film *Martin the Cobbler*, based on the book *Where Love Is, There God Is Also*, by Leo Tolstoy.

Martin is not a friend of God, having lost his wife and then his only son. A holy man comes to his shop looking for a new leather binding for his Bible, but Martin is reluctant to take the job.

"God and I are not getting along," laments Martin.

"Read the book," exhorts the holy man as he departs.

Martin reads, and in the midst of reading hears God speak.

"Martin! Martin! Look out your window in the morning, for I am coming to you."

Not sure if the voice is revelation or delusion, Martin nonetheless looks out the small window in his lonely shop. He sees a cold street sweeper whom he welcomes in for a cup of tea. He sees a shivering mother and her baby whom he ushers inside to get warm. He sees "Granny" scolding a young boy for stealing an apple from her basket, and he rushes outside to mediate a peaceful resolve.

Still, as the sun descends, God has not come to a despondent Martin.

Then, all of a sudden, God speaks again.

"Martin, do you not know me?"

"Who are you?" Martin calls out.

Then, in a vision, Martin sees the street sweeper, the mother and baby, the boy and the grandmother and God says:

"It is I!"

"It is I!"

"It is I!"

Ron Rolheiser, OMI, in his marvelous book *The Holy Longing*, reminds us: "The most important things God wants to say to us are not given in extraordinary mystical visions. The God of the incarnation has real flesh on earth and speaks to us in the bread and butter of our lives through things that have skin—historical circumstances, our families, our neighbors, our churches" (page 95).

As God challenged Martin, I challenged my students to "look out" the window of their lives and see in a new way. Instead of expecting God's Revelation to happen in extraordinary events, start seeing ordinary events with new eyes. I gave a few examples and a motivational pep talk. Then I sent them on a mission to "meet God today."

The result is this book.

All the words are the students'. I simply added a comma, corrected a misspelled word, broke a long paragraph in two, or made a few other small grammatical alterations.

When they handed in their work, I was surprised, inspired, and uplifted.

Eschewing an overload of adjectives and redundant information, my students wrote with refreshing brevity and heartfelt candor. Some entries seem more poetry than prose—and prayerful.

This is a book of young teenage glimpses of transcendence. But it is also about transcendence itself. This is a book about God. I consider myself exceedingly fortunate to assist youth in seeing the more, the beyond, and the reality beneath the appearance of things. "The best and most beautiful things in the world cannot be seen or even touched," wrote the mystic Helen Keller, "they must be felt within the heart." How delightful is the heart of the thirteen-year-old.

Having assigned this project for nearly two decades, I can say, as I read these entries, "I met God today."

I hope you do too.

—Danny Brock, general editor

I Met God in
My Family

"The God who has become incarnate in human flesh is found, first and foremost, not in meditation and monasteries, albeit God is found there, but in our homes."

—Ronald Rolheiser, priest, speaker, and spiritual author

Artist for this chapter

Alexandrea
Delos Reyes

I met God today in my parents.

My mom was making dinner and my dad went up to her and hugged her from behind and he said, "I love you."

That day I saw all the love that keeps their marriage strong and full of the life God blessed them with.

—Paige Scholes

My dad was always a little more religious than the average Joe. He also had great values that I believe everybody should have.

One day, after a muddy soccer game, Dad came to pick me up in his Mercedes. I said, "Do you have a towel or something to put over the seat so it doesn't get muddy?"

Dad replied, "Gaurav, I can replace the seat, and even the car, but I cannot replace you, so you are more important."

That day I saw God in my dad,

and I do so every time I see him.

—Gaurav Sekhon

I saw God in my dad today.

My parents are divorced, so we see him on the weekends usually. I know it's hard for him to be alone all the time, so whenever he gets the chance to see us he really gets excited.

One weekend me and my brother were really sick and we told our dad we couldn't come over. He said that he didn't care and that we had to get ready in 15 minutes. So we did and came over to his apartment.

We both took a nap when we arrived. When I woke up I asked my dad what the purpose was of our coming over if we were sleeping the whole time. He said just seeing our beautiful faces made him happy.

—E. Reda

I met God when my grandmother died.

Her favorite season was fall. She loved the autumn colors. The reds and oranges and yellows.

On the first day of fall, she died. Whenever I see the autumn colors or the leaves falling, I think of her.

—Cassidy A. McDonald

One night before bed, my mom and I were having a conversation about weddings and all that they involve. We were talking about wedding dresses, when out of nowhere my mom took a dusty old box out of the closet and opened it. Inside was a large black and gold book full of my parents' wedding pictures.

We looked through all of these pictures that I had never seen before, and it made me feel happy about how much they love each other.

The box is now just sitting in my room, which is unlike my mom because she usually puts things away after she pulls them out of the closet. This makes me feel like it has been handed off to me so I can always cherish it.

I meet God every day through my parents!

—Jessica Coady

I met God in my sister Grace.

I think her kindergarten class was doing a unit on Monarch butterflies in science. She came to me and handed me a card with a giant butterfly on it. I didn't really care for it, and I didn't even open it up until a week later. It had the cutest poem in it about never hurting any living thing. On the back it said, "I love you Meghan. You are one of the best sisters ever."

Out of all four sisters I have, Grace is the one who looks up to me the most and wants to do exactly everything I do. From things like doin make-up, going to the mall, having her own cell phone, and going to Starbucks. She can always be the sweetest—yet most annoying too.

But, I love my sister and I hope she stays the caring, affectionate sweetheart she currently is now.

—Meghan McQuay

13

I met God in my grandmother.

My grandmother's name was Elizabeth Farrell. She has got to be the holiest person that I have ever met. She was the mother of seven children, all of whom she dedicated her life to.

From all of the stories my mother has told me, and from meeting her and talking to her, I know for sure that she is a very holy person. She said the Rosary every day, and went to church every Sunday until she wasn't able to anymore. She called each one of her children every day to ask how they were doing.

Since we live in Victoria and she lived in Newfoundland we weren't with her very often, but I know she prayed for us very often. As if she wasn't holy enough, she passed away on Easter Sunday.

—Jessica Coady

When I was unloading the dishwasher, my dad came from behind me and hugged me, and kissed me on the head saying, "I love you."

I saw God in my dad that day.

—Daniel K.

The first time I met God was when I was four years old. My little sister, two at the time, and I walked to a park about two or three blocks away from our house. At the time I thought I had total independence, just Kate and I going to Beckwith Park. But actually my Dad was following us the entire time. Giving us independence but keeping us safe.

I didn't know he did that until a few weeks ago, but that small act of making us feel "like big girls" made me so happy. My sister and I played there for hours, playing on the monkey bars and building sand castles.

That day I met God in my father.

—Kelly

I met God in my brother,

which is really weird and abnormal.

My little brother does prayers every night. I decided to take part in it for the sake of it.

We fight non-stop every day. I try to stop fighting but he gets really annoying. Anyways, while we were praying, he prayed for everyone—even me! Then I remembered that God forgave people even though they didn't believe in him or hurt him. He gave his life for us. He prayed for people and helped everyone.

So, in a way, my brother was God for a night!

—Brianna Teixeira

This afternoon I went to the park with my little sister, Persaya. Our family is friends with the family that lives across from the park, and they have two children that like to play with Persaya.

When I went with Persaya to ask the children of the family to play, I saw the excitement and hopeful look on her face when we knocked on the door. I realized how much children care about the little things that most adults just take for granted—same with teens.

Later on, when Persaya and her friend were playing, I just sat and observed her happiness from afar. It warmed me and made me smile.

I met God through my sister's happiness.

—Kinaydah R.

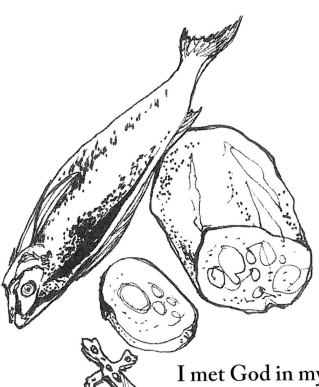

I met God in my grandpa.

Since I was little my grandpa always took me to Sunday Mass and would teach me about our religion and history. I always looked up to him—he never made mistakes it seemed. He would take me fishing and halfway through we would stop and say a prayer for fish if we didn't have any or to thank God for the fish we had caught.

My grandpa always tells me stories about the saints and keeps me up-to-date with church politics. I've always thought of him as a role model.

Most of his free time he spends helping the poor or in our church. He once told me that God asked him to give half his time and half his money to the less fortunate and to charity.

—Connor O'N.

I met God today, and every time my mom and dad look into each other's eyes. When they do you can feel the love they have for each other.

It's like God showing me how great they are for each other and how great they are for me.

—Jamie Christie

My past experience of God was when I celebrated my grandmother's eightieth birthday with my whole family. My family is so kind and caring, I saw God in all of them.

But of all my family,

I saw God the most in my grandma.

My grandmother is very kind and is strong in her faith. She is very thoughtful of all her children and grandchildren. She has a very close connection with God and is at peace with the world.

—Mahisha C.

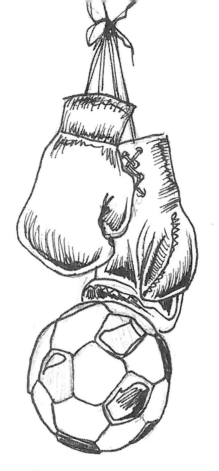

I met God today in my grandpa.

He is seventy-eight years old, and yet he is always up for taking care of me, and driving me wherever. This is what God would do. He is probably one of my favorite people in the world, and I love him.

Also, he is one of the most accomplished people that I have met. He was a runner (the fastest in Ireland), a bouncer, a boxer, a soccer player, a soccer coach, and the nicest person in the world.

—Dan Polson

Today I met God in my older cousin.

My cousin is a very self-centered kind of guy that only cares about himself and nobody else.

One afternoon he and I decided to go to the Bay Centre downtown. Before entering the Bay Centre on the corner of the street was this homeless woman and her baby. Both were crying. In my experience of him he would always make fun of homeless people. Instead of making fun of her, he crouched down and wiped her tears and the baby's tears. Then he gave them a twenty-dollar bill. He got up and kept on walking but I stood there with my mouth wide open. I could not believe that I just saw the self-centered guy do something that was not self-centered at all.

I met God in him because he inspired me to be a better person and I believe that God inspires me to be a better person as well.

—Paneet A.

Today I met God in my memories of my Opa (Grandfather).

My Opa was a hard working gardener who had a passion for dahlias and was always willing to give a helping hand. He was always friendly and cheerful and always wore a smile on his face.

On February 24th, God needed a gardener in Heaven and called for the best!

Unfortunately, I lost my Opa after his courageous battle with lymphoma. I will always admire my Opa, as he was a great role model and someone I looked up to.

—Greg Van Dyk

I met God in a holy person, my dad.

My dad is one of the greatest people I know. Besides the fact of him taking me to a PG-13 movie when I was seven, teaching me how to fish, putting on the best puppet shows ever, and taking me to McDonalds but telling my mom we had salad, he is probably the reason I have such trust in God.

He taught me the power of prayer, he read me the Bible, and he has such an inspirational story, it shows me how much God loves him.

—Emily B.

**I met God today
in my father.
My Daddy.**

My friend texted me one day telling me
that she was committing suicide.

I cried and was paralyzed, unable to
move. Somehow, my dad came home just in
time to see the text, and call an ambulance
to her house.

I saw God in him that day, and I
continue to see a savior in him.

—Alexandrea DR

Today I met God through my mother.

I have been fully enlightened on how deep a mother's love goes. It may seem hard to be an adolescent but it must be even harder to take care of your "precious, little one." I can only imagine how much responsibility and stress a mother has.

To be a mom you'd have to be filled with so much love, you'd almost burst. Thank you for making me realize how much my mother loves me.

—Chanel Mandap

I met God today when my dad told me that he loved me.

I can't even remember the last time I heard him say those words to anyone, so hearing him say them to me meant a lot. It was like God talked to me through my dad and wanted to tell me that no matter what, he still loves me.

After I heard my dad say that, I started to tear up because he's never said it to me and I was starting to wish he would tell me, and then he did.

—Felicity Goodfellow

I met God today through my family.

My family and I went out to eat lunch. Later, we went to the beach and talked. I felt good and loved, especially since my mom took time off work to spend time with me and the family. I felt really happy and grateful to have such a loving family!

We spent the rest of the day at my aunt's house and I saw how happy my mom and dad were. They didn't look as stressed out as they usually were and it was good to see that they were happy.

It was good knowing that God gave us a day for leisure time. I find that Sundays are the most joyous times of the week.

—Amanda Do

It was Valentine's Day and my dad wasn't home yet. My mom, sister, and I sat in the living room waiting for him.

A couple of minutes later my dad came through the side door. He walked into the living room holding a bouquet of roses and a small cake. He set the cake onto the table and walked over to my mom and gave her the roses. Then he said, "I love you."

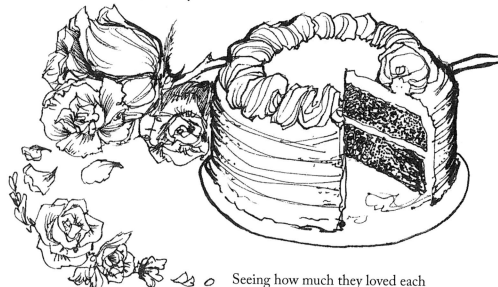

Seeing how much they loved each other reminded me of how much

God loves us too.

—Alyssa Mariano

It was probably 6 p.m. when I dozed out. I had an argument with my parents about going to a birthday party, and I decided to go to my room and just cool down.

I had a dream that I was at home but I couldn't find anybody. So I went outside to see if they were there but they weren't. So I called their cells and it said no one had those numbers. I ran to every house to see if anyone knew where my family was, but every house was empty.

I woke up frightened and needed to find out if it was reality. I ran upstairs and found my parents and my siblings. I gave them a big hug and apologized. **I think God was trying to tell me** that I needed my family and that they just do things because they care about me.

—Alyssa Mariano

I Met God in
People

"Faith sees God's face in every human face."
—Catherine Doherty, Catholic social worker and author

Artist for this chapter

Paula Cota

I met God today through some kids I saw on the bus.

The children were holding on to their mother as they were sleeping. I could see the love in the mother's eyes as she looked down at her children.

—Miri Chavarria

I met God today while I was walking home from school and I saw two little boys and their mom walking along.

The two boys started to run, with their mom walking quickly behind them. In the little boys' faces I saw joy and no fear of falling or getting hit by a car. They were trouble free, not worrying about what people think or how they looked. I wished for a trouble-less and comfortable lifestyle like these two boys.

It was in their faces that I met God.

—Mollie M.

I met God today through a person I was playing badminton with at Spectrum. This is because after the game he said, "Good job," and "Thanks for the game!"

I think that was pretty neat because even though he lost the game, he was still happy and not a bad sport.

I will try to be like him in the future and not to be mad if I lose.

—Dominic Henderson

I met God today in the elderly couple

who were walking down the street together. They looked so happy talking to each other and holding hands.

As I was watching them, they got to a busy street, and when it was time to cross, the old man, being the gentleman, helped his wife down, and they crossed the street together.

I thought it was the sweetest thing ever, of course me being the sucker for cute romances. But that couple reminded me what true love looks like even though they were old.

—D. Niswar

Today I met God in a total stranger.

I was in line to buy something at Starbucks with my friend. We were kind of in a hurry but luckily there was only one other person in line. He was covered in tattoos and was wearing low pants and a big hoodie.

Immediately, I thought, oh my, what a creeper, and made sure not to stand too close. He must have noticed we were in a hurry because he said, "Go right ahead of me." We quickly ordered our drinks and realized that we didn't have enough money. We cancelled our order and left to go wait for her dad.

But later the cashier came out also, with the two drinks we ordered. The creepy man had paid for them. I felt so bad for judging him before, and we went to go say thank you but he was already gone. He was the last person I would expect to do a random act of kindness and not even ask for recognition. I must never judge someone like that again.

—Paula Cota

Today I was having some trouble with some science homework. I asked my friend if she can explain it to me. She tried but I still didn't understand.

Miss Taft was walking down the hall while my friend was trying to explain it to me. I guess she heard that I didn't understand it because she stopped to help me. She explained it until I understood the question.

After Miss Taft left, I said to my friend, "Wow, Miss Taft is so nice."

That day I met God in Miss Taft.

—Tiffany

I met God today while walking my dogs after school.

I noticed this elderly couple going on a walk too. On the first view I knew I saw God. I saw their love. I was walking past them when they stopped mid-step to talk to me. After chatting to them about my dogs, the conversation started. We began to talk about their marriage.

It just so happened that it was their sixty-first anniversary they were celebrating that day. It was adorable how they said that they didn't need a big celebration but only to have each other's company. They were reunited high school lovers who just wanted to live the last years they had left to the fullest. Henry, the man, had just recently been diagnosed with stage-three lung cancer.

I found it funny to have met such an open couple who would tell a teenager their whole life story. I guess it was because we connected. Don't ever judge some people too early.

—Kirsten Suesser

I was at the grocery store picking up something for supper when I noticed a single mother walk in with four kids. They weren't being too helpful but rather quite picky about the foods they ate. Not one kid could agree with another so their mom just thought she would buy it all.

I was still shopping with my mom when I saw them walk up to the cash register. I couldn't hear the conversation between them but the mother was trying to say she didn't have enough money for all of it after her card had been declined. That's when a man behind her spoke up and said, "Don't worry, this bill is on me." He saved her the embarrassment of pulling items out of her cart, and paid for her whole bill . . . a total of $25.50!

People and incidents like this, that show the kindness and **consideration of others, are God's message.**

—Kirsten Suesser

When I was in third grade, I was really sick. Whenever I would eat or drink something, I would throw up. So one day my mom took me to the hospital where the doctors gave me fluids since I couldn't eat or drink anything.

I saw God in those doctors

and nurses because they took really good care of me and gave me everything I needed. I am also thankful to my dad who stayed at the hospital with me the whole time.

—Saavin S.V.

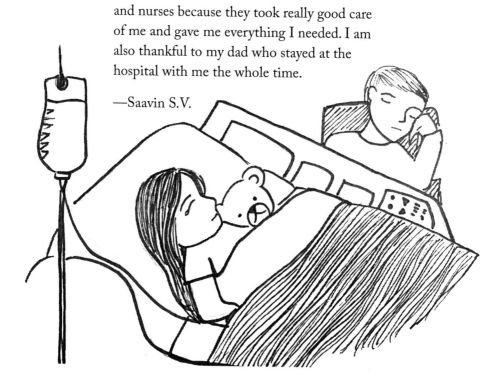

I met God in a holy person.

The holy person who influenced my life forever was Father Keith. Father Keith is the most kind, loving person I have ever met (aside from my mom). Father Keith is like a saint.

He used to teach religion to grades four and under at my old school, and everyone who met him loved him. He is always smiling and is super generous to everyone, from little kids to grown men. His religion classes were always fun while at the same time very informative. He is like an angel on earth.

I met God in him from when I first met him. His love for everyone is so unbelievable that it makes you wonder, Is that what God is like?

Father Keith is now retired, but he will always be in everyone's hearts.

—David E.

My past experience of God happened when I was on the bus with my Nona.

It was very crowded on the bus, so we had to stand in the aisle and hold onto the back of someone's seat. There was a boy, probably in his early twenties, sitting down in the seat beside us. He had dreadlocks, tattoos, and piercings everywhere. He noticed that my Nona looked tired, and offered her his seat.

I met God in someone who I least expected. He did a small thing, but it had a big impact on me and my Nona, and it brightened up our day.

—Julie F.

I
found
God
today
in
Annie.

I don't have many Catholic friends,
but Annie is one of the few. Talking
to her is different because we share
similar morals and values. I feel I can
talk to her about my faith without
being judged.

—G

I saw God today in my classmate.

She, somehow, saw the pain beneath
my fake smiles and giggles, and suddenly
pulled me into a hug. I looked at her as tears welled in
my eyes, as she sat me down on a nearby chair, as she
comforted me.

I told her my story as she listened, and she opened
up to me with her secrets too. I'm so glad to call her
my close and true friend now.

I'm really thankful that God put her in my life.

—Alexandrea DR

I met God today in a bus driver.

As soon as the bell rang, all the kids taking the early bus ran outside to catch it. It came earlier than usual, and it was already at the stop as we ran up to the crosswalk.

That day I had a lot of homework, a test to study for and a soccer practice. I was stressed out that I wouldn't have enough time to do everything if I had to wait another 30 minutes for the next bus to come. Usually, the bus driver would just drive away, but this time he didn't and he waited for the light to change so all of us made it onto the bus. I met God in that bus driver because he was nice and waited for us, and I didn't have to stress out anymore.

—Bridget Mateyko

I met God today in a simple but interesting way.

I was eating lunch with my friends and someone told a joke and we all started laughing. It hit me how lucky I am to have such great friends. I realized that my whole life I have taken friends for granted. It wasn't until today I realized and appreciated how lucky I am.

Friends are a true gift from God.

—Connor O'N.

The last day before Christmas break I was going to get on the bus in the morning to go to school. The bus driver was standing in front of the bus handing out candy canes to everybody that boarded the bus.

This stood out to me because the bus I take in the morning is only ever a single decker, and is the most crowded bus you will ever take. Being around a bunch of tired, bitter people every day, you'd think that would rub off on him. It never does.

I met God in my bus driver.

—Jenna Frank

I met God today in the film about Mother Teresa.

She reminded me of Jesus. She was almost like Jesus, but a female, a female Jesus.

She was loving and humble and helped anyone she could. In this film, she inspired me to help others as well. Maybe one day, I could travel around the world helping others. And it was only because of Mother Teresa, that this thought came to mind.

—Gloria

I met God through a friend.

I was going through a really, really rough time and I wanted to just give up. I think that friend was the only person, the only thing that kept me going. They would always check up on me to see how I was doing. We would talk about it and that really helped. I think they were the only person willing to listen to my lengthy tangents.

So to that friend, who is reading this or listening to this, you know who you are, thank you.

—Brett F.

I saw God today in a man on the bus.

I took my usual bus from school to Saint Joseph's and then waited for my second bus to pick me up. When I got on the bus, I sat across from a man who seemed about thirty-five years old, and a young child who seemed to be six. The man had tons of tattoos and a nose piercing and I thought to myself, "That's the type of person who shouldn't be a parent."

But as the bus ride continued, I saw how deeply the man cared for his son. He asked him about his day and made sure he was sitting down when the bus was moving. When they got off, the father held his child's hand and helped him down the step.

I thought to myself, "How stupid was I to judge a book by its cover." I think God meant that to be a lesson for me to not judge people by their appearance.

—Kaitlyn Chan

I met God today in people I don't even know.

So I was walking down a busy street with lots of people. Being me, I always smile at others. Then I started making eye contact with a bunch of people, and they all smiled back. I felt so good.

Every time a person smiled at me, I felt a big bubble of happiness arise inside me, and they all made me feel special with their beautiful smiles. I think even a smile can make a difference in a person.

—D. Niswar

I Met God in *Creation*

"Let's not allow life to pass us by while we ignore the signals of divine revelation that come through ordinary and extraordinary moments."

—Joyce Rupp, religious sister, speaker, and spiritual author

Artist for this chapter

Gloria Wong

My family went on a trip along the Sunshine Coast for twelve days. We had a blast! We stopped to see the scenery and major tourist attractions. But one day we went for a kayak adventure with a guide. He was so nice. Anyway, once we were all set up and ready to go, we slowly drifted off.

Our guide guided us along the rocky cliffs to look down beside us and see many different kinds of starfish. That was a terrific sight.

Well, my point is, that when we were on that trip, on that very day, I realized how beautiful the world is and how much fun it was to spray my family with pumps of seawater!

That's when I saw God, or at least felt him around me. I loved that day, because I felt like I really belonged in the world.

—Stephanie Crighton

He came to me not through a book or the sky but through one of his creatures.

A swan.

We were canoeing on a lake and it was a sunny but foggy morning and there wasn't anybody or anything around.

Then, out of the fog, came a swan and it swam to the centre of the sunshine. It stopped and flapped its wings, spraying water droplets everywhere. But since the sun was shining, it looked like gold.

A simple but beautiful animal showed me how

God can be just about anywhere at any time.

—Chelsea T.

I met God today in my backyard.

I barely ever look back there, but today I did and
it reminded me how pretty it actually is. There
were daisies growing all over the grass. The trees
were in blossom and the birds were singing. It's
kind of hard to describe what it looked like in that
moment, but I was just amazed by the beauty God
has created around us and how little we notice it.
It's like my art teacher says, "You can always
see a little of the artist in the artwork."

—G.

A pair of robins started building a nest in a tree outside our kitchen window. It is fun to watch them collect twigs and items for their nest. Today I saw one of them finding bugs and worms to eat. Soon there will be baby birds.

I look forward to seeing the baby robins and watching what happens.

God is great.

—Max

I was at my horseback riding barn today when I encountered God. It is so peaceful there! You can see the deer jumping through the pasture and can hear the birds sing and the crickets chirp. And it is there where the best and most favorable creatures live . . . horses!

Often if I'm going through a tough time, I just escape to go see one of them. I have grown a deep connection with one of the horses. His name is Dusty and he's a twenty-one-year-old Morgan . . . but he sure as heck doesn't act his age! Whenever I see him I snuggle my head into his neck and shoulder and he turns his muzzle in and wraps me. This whole experience I've done too many times to count, but it's still effective and relaxes me all the time. The scenery, as well, is quite something.

Sometimes after my barn chores are finished, I go climb a big boulder and look out at the rolling hills, nature, animals, etc., and find a state of relaxation when nothing can stress me out; my worries being wiped away. There I can contemplate questions I never had the time to think about before.

It's important for everyone to have a time like that at some point in their day or week. God's creations, and other contributions, make me relaxed and I can find peace here . . .

. . . and I thank God for that.

—Kirsten Suesser

I live right beside a park. When I was younger, if I was mad at my parents, I would "run away" to the park. I found this rock, up high, and it seemed like I could see the world from up there and nobody would be able to see or find me when I was there.

I'd usually stay there for 20 minutes and by then I'd be crazy calm, like Buddha! I think, looking back, that there was a bit of God in that spot that stopped my temper from getting the best of me. I thought I was alone up there, but **God was with me the whole time.**

—Ava Zanatta

My past experience of God was when I was going through a very hard time. I felt sad, alone, and depressed. I was very confused, so I went outside to be alone. I climbed a cherry blossom tree and sat on a branch near the top, just staring at the view. I took a few shaky breaths and tried to sort my thoughts.

Suddenly, I felt calm. It was like all my negative emotions were muted. It was like when you put your head underwater, and you can still hear, but everything feels far away. It's hard to explain, but I felt peaceful. My problems seemed so small and insignificant compared to those of our world. I felt small, not in a bad way, just the world seemed so huge.

—Lily V.

Today
I met
God
through
a bird.

Today I pointed out a bird gathering materials for a nest. I realized that the only reason it was building the nest was for their babies.

Birds go out of their way to care for their babies. This helped me realize all the things my parents do for me, and how much they love me.

—Harrison

I met God today
in the golden sunlight
that shone into my kitchen
this morning.

It reminded me that Monday mornings are not awful, that the gold light highlighted the flowers and trees outside, as if saying, "Be thankful for me."

It was a nice moment and made me feel positive for the rest of the day. Such a small sign, but it did make a difference oddly enough.

—Camille

I Met God in
My Faith

"In the days ahead, you will either be a mystic (one who has experienced God for real) or nothing at all."

—Karl Rahner, priest and theologian

Artist for this chapter

Chanel Mandap

I always seem
to meet God
in the people who
spread the Good News.

Whether it's a priest, a religion teacher, or just an ordinary human being.

They make me feel good when they talk about an amazing person who walked the earth two thousand years ago.

I can't imagine a world without religion, or without anyone to preach it.

—Seamus Ryan-Lloyd

My family is pretty religious, so my parents include/drag me to things such as talks from priests, or the Stations of the Cross every Friday of Lent.

I usually complain and whine about it, I mean what teenager wants to go to that? But after I go I always feel the exact opposite of what I was feeling before.

—Ania Z.

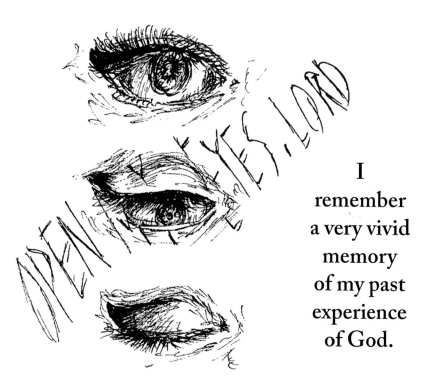

I remember a very vivid memory of my past experience of God.

It was in grade five.

We were having a Mass and Reconciliation. At the end of Mass, we had the opportunity to go to Confession. At the time, I was very disconnected from my family because I used to fight with them a lot. I decided to go to Confession to see what it was like.

The priest told me to confess my sins, and when I did, I ended up crying. I felt overwhelmed and relieved, like a weight had been lifted off my shoulders. I truly felt like my sins were forgiven. I felt like I could change and act better towards my family. I genuinely felt like God gave me forgiveness and strength. It was an indescribable feeling that changed my life with God and my family.

—Amanda Do

I met God when I went into Confession with Father

Paul. When I went into the confessional, I felt heavy (with sins). When I told the priest all my sins, I felt empty and light (without sin). In that moment God said to me, "Go, and sin no more."

That's where I met God.

—Martin Vargas

I met God about a year ago when I went to the Golden Temple in India. The reason why I met God there is because it was so peaceful. Right when I got there it felt like everything just stopped. There was no sound of cars, no sound of car horns, only the sound of the hymns that the priests were singing.

Also I could feel the presence of God there like he was there with us. It was the best feeling ever knowing that God was there with me. I know if I ever get the chance to go there again and be with God, I will.

—Vardeep G.

I met God today at church.

Although church can sometimes seem very boring and the priest goes on forever about things that I don't understand, today it really clicked for me.

As I looked at Jesus on the cross, God just came to me and I felt totally peaceful and calm. I started to realize that He was all around me, sitting in the pews. He was my family, my friends, strangers, and relatives. Suddenly everything the priest said made sense, and I understood it all. When I went up to receive the Eucharist, I knew that it was the Body and Blood of Christ, not just ordinary bread and wine.

I believe that I experienced a true encounter with God today that I will never forget. Thank You God.

—Laura Walzak

I met God, during spring break, in a priest.

His name was Father Terry. I met God in the homily which was about how fathers should be the person to bring faith into the family. He should not just step down and let the mother or no one spread the faith in the family.

Also, he mentioned how everyone should go to church as much as possible, at least every Sunday, for our Savior told us to.

This means so much to me because I was with my cousins and auntie who rarely ever go to church because they are "too busy." And my uncle doesn't ever come to church though he was married in a church. It made me realize how fortunate I am to have a whole family who goes to church every Sunday. And I have a father who shares our faith with us.

—Jill

I see God at the Sikh Temple

because it is very peaceful there. People are not allowed to talk or make noise because that is their time to connect with God. I see people with their eyes closed trying to connect with God.

—Saavin S. V.

When I was little my dad, who is
in the military, would leave a lot and
I would have to move to different
countries. I was always upset when
my dad left and when I had to say
goodbye to my friends.

When I moved I would always
feel lonely and I felt like I had no
friends. **But I always had God
at my side,** as my friend. He was
always by my side. He was always
there for me when my dad couldn't be.

—Camille Ouellet

When I was six years old, I had finally got the bravery to sleep by myself. This was a really big deal because now my entire family would think of me as brave and mature.

The first night I was completely terrified. A week passed and I still felt the same way. Then one night my mother gave me the advice to pray before I went to sleep. During prayer I asked God to protect me every night for the rest of my life. This was the greatest idea I had ever had because every night I felt like God would be with me after praying.

To this very day I pray before I go to sleep because after praying I feel the presence of **God is right beside me through the entire night.**

—Paneet A.

I met God in my religion when I took a pilgrimage to the holy city of Mecca.

I was oh so ever lucky to get to do that, and I am glad I got to go because it was life-changing.

As soon as we got there we went to visit the Ka'bah, which was in the biggest mosque in the world. When I first saw it, tears were slowly coming down my face, and the others around me were bawling, and I felt really awkward. Then I looked around at the people and the mosque, trying to take it all in, because it was a dream come true for me.

I finally got to be in the place that I have been talking and hearing about for many years.

—D. Niswar

I met God today in a holy person, Pope Francis.

Before, I hardly understood a Pope's value. Since he was appointed Pope, he spread his humbleness. He preaches directly from God as he accepts all people.

Pope Francis is selfless and has humanity. Pope Francis taught me the importance of his gifts with his God-given grace and value.

—Chanel Mandap

I met God in my church.

It was a normal Sunday morning at church. The priest had just done his homily. The church was quiet and everyone was focused in prayer. It was then when I recognized God was with me.

The stained glass let light enter and the birds were overjoyed with song. This experience let me feel so close to God, a feeling that I have never felt (or at least never this strong). I then really understood that God isn't just in church with me, he lives inside of me so I can feel this connection to Him all the time.

I don't know how to put it in words, but the feeling doesn't need an explanation anyways. I then learned more about the Christian/Catholic part of me that God introduced.

—Kirsten Suesser

I always meet God when I go to church.

I can tell Him my problems
and requests in complete
silence. I love the fact that I
can feel my problems going
away, even just after an
hour. I think Mass is one of
the highlights of my week.

—Seamus Ryan-Lloyd

I met God today in religion class.

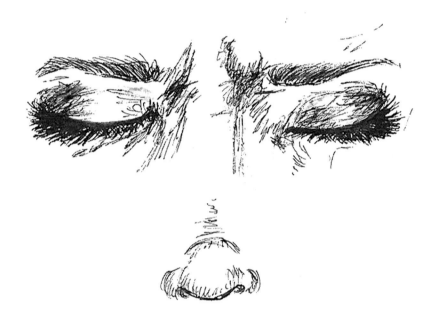

It was the last class of the day, to be more specific a really bad stressful day.

Our religion teacher let us relax for about 15 minutes in the dark with peaceful relaxing ocean noises/music. This was very calming and after closing my eyes I was taken back to some of my happiest, most amazing and relaxing days.

Though this may not seem like a big deal, this music and relaxing time made my day better and made my mood much happier.

I met God in the peace and tranquility I felt.

—Mollie M.

I met God today by going to adoration.

It's called "Hora Santa," which means "Holy Hour." It's an hour of singing and praising God, basically just letting God love you. Sometimes it gets emotional because the lyrics are so beautiful.

I met God when, while a song was playing, I saw angels around the host. That's where I saw God.

—Martin Vargas

I don't know if this really counts, but **I met God today in Pope Francis.** I've obviously never met him, but you do hear quite a lot about him. I'd just been reading about him and the wonderful things he does. He sounds like such an amazing person.

He gives freely, he serves selflessly, and he loves unreservedly. He doesn't just preach the faith, he lives it, and he lives it with passion.

Pope Francis inspires me to give love and kindness more freely, and I see God in him.

—G.

My mom is really strict about going to church, and she makes me go every Sunday. I altar serve, and she does children's liturgy.

She woke me up to get ready and I was grumpy because I had to serve and I had already served for three weeks in a row. It wasn't supposed to be like that, but people didn't show up, so I was always asked to fill in. On top of all that, it was raining outside.

We went to church and I served, and during the middle of Mass my anger and annoyance faded away. By the end of church, when I walked outside, the sun was shining and there was a rainbow in the sky.

Being in church with all the happy singing and praising had changed my mood. **I met God at church** that day because He turned my gray skies to blue.

—Jenna B.

When Father Al gave us that tour of the church, I saw God.

Father Al is old-ish, he has a pretty prominent accent, but despite that, he has one of the most wonderful faces, smiles, and twinkly eyes.

You can see God in Father Al's smile.

—Ava Zanatta

I met God in a holy person.

This was the time when they chose the new Pope. I don't remember it well, I was not interested. I was probably going through a hard time. But when I heard that the new Pope was from Latin America, I started paying attention. And then I discovered his new name was Francis, basically Francisco. I got happy all of a sudden.

—Francisco H. D.

This experience of God wasn't actually today, but last night.

I was in bed at the time, and it was about 11:30 so I couldn't write it down. Here is the experience as best I can remember.

I was praying to God as I do every night, and I started to think about how a lot of the time when I'm praying it feels as though I've picked up the phone and dialed the number. It's ringing, but nobody is answering. I started wondering what God wanted me to do with my life. I was still praying, and as I asked this question, I believe God helped me reflect on my actions.

I came to a realization that, at least for now, **God was calling me to spread his love** in the little things I do. Whether it be just a smile, or a held door, I would be spreading his love.

This story may not be the most profound or inspiring, but for me, I think it will have a big impact on my life.

—Cecilia

An important past experience I've had with God was when I was in my first adoration. I was at Saint Joseph's Church and it was beautiful. There were tea light candles around the altar, and they glowed like stars. It was on the "Rise and Shine" retreat, which was the most holy and fun retreat I ever went on.

—Jacob Carty

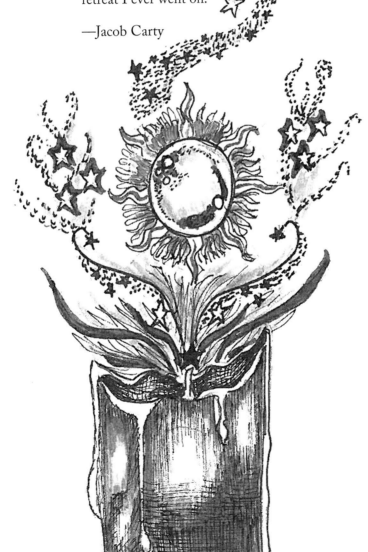

I met God today in my church.

Yesterday was actually Easter, so . . . yeah . . . when our family went to Mass that day, it was packed. I've never ever seen so many people in our church before. Half of us were standing and half of us were sitting!

Most people seemed pretty bothered by that. I thought it was amazing. It is incredible that so many people were there together, all at the same time, to celebrate the Resurrection of Jesus Christ. It is outstanding to me.

—Kinaydah R.

Some time ago I was invited on a trip to Hawaii with some friends. We went for two weeks and stayed in a house that consisted of a pool, gym, outdoor shower, etc. My point is, it was very nice and I would have never thought I would get homesick. The thought didn't even cross my mind.

But about a week in, I started to feel sad and vulnerable. Nothing seemed to help. I just wanted to go home.

Then one evening, I was on the phone with my mom and she said, **"Go to a quiet place and ask God for some guidance."** Thinking it wasn't going to help, I still did it and was shocked by the results. The next day I was happy and could enjoy the rest of the experience with my friends.

—Mya Macleod

I met God today at the Ash Wednesday service when Father Rolf was talking about the breath of God and how we need God to survive. I felt suddenly strong and uplifted and I wondered why God chooses to put His breath of life into us.

And then I realized that it is God's unconditional love for us that makes Him love us, but I couldn't understand that either.

I think that unconditional love is something we humans cannot fully understand, not because it is complex, but because it is very simple. And that perfect simplicity is something only truly understood by God.

—Raya MacKenzie

I met God in my religion.

I thought about this for a very long time. Honestly, this was one of the hardest things to do in this booklet for me.

I am not really a religious person other than religion class and school Mass. I don't really think or do any religious things. So for this booklet I decided to try and be more religious.

I would pray to God if I was scared or unsure and needed help. I also read a story in the Bible. The one where Jesus reveals himself and Thomas doesn't believe until he sees it. I haven't read much of the Bible in a long time and it surprised me how easy it was to read. I expected like ancient dialogue ("where are thou Jesus" and stuff).

I met God by opening up and experiencing my religion.

—Jaeden Adams

I Met God in . . .

"God is addressing us in all moments of life. . . . That this revelatory power is more apparent in some moments than others is due more to our own openness and readiness than to the intensity and availability of God's saving presence."

—Joseph F. Schmidt, Christian Brother, counselor, and spiritual author

Artist for this chapter

Gloria Wong

I meet God whenever
I play guitar.

Whenever I pick up my guitar
and play, all the stress and
problems in my life go away. I
need that time to step away from
all the commotion in life, and for
me, playing guitar does that.

I think God is comforting me
through my guitar.

—Harrison

Today
I found God
in a
Disney movie.

We were on a long car ride with my family and they had already seen it up to a thousand times, but somewhere around the fiftieth time watching it I kind of realized what the message was.

Life is an adventure. It's great to dream and make plans for the future, but not so much that you miss the world that is going on around you.

The old man in the movie feels bad for not taking his wife to see the waterfall, but he actually took her on a much better adventure than that. I think that the real adventure of life is the relationships we have with other people, and it's so easy to lose sight of the things we have and the people that are around us until they're gone. I really realize how lucky I am to know someone before they either move or pass away.

So, if you don't kind of wake up a little bit and go, "Wow, I've got some really cool stuff around me every day," and then thank God for the cool stuff you have already instead of dreaming up some other cool stuff, you will spend your life pleading for an adventure without realizing you were living in one the whole time.

So thank God for the movie *Up*.

—Paula Cota

One experience of God I will never forget

is watching the "One World Show" put on by Pearson College. The college is international, and it takes people from all over the world (over a hundred different countries) who are working hard toward peace and harmony in the world. The show is put on by these people, and is so inspiring.

Just seeing this makes me realize that those people are the perfect example of how God intended us to live. I feel that God is behind that show, helping the performers and sending them to deliver a great message.

—David E.

I felt God's presence with me today in my room.

I got into a fight with my parents and was in no mood to forgive. I was extremely frustrated and full of anger.

Suddenly it all went away. It felt as if a wind had passed through me, blowing away all my bad emotions.

After that I apologized to my parents and knew that God helped me do it.

—Maeve P.

I met God today

when my mom showed
me a story she found on
Facebook. It started with
a video a couple made who
wanted to adopt a baby. The
couple was not able to have
a baby of their own.

In the song they sang about
how much they wanted a baby
and how they would try their
best to be great parents. The video was
shared by many people and a birth mother chose the
couple to adopt her son.

This story made my mom so happy. She said it was a
true gift of love for the birth mother to give her child to
this couple to adopt. My uncle is adopted and my mom
is thankful every day to have a brother.

—Max

I
met
God
today
in
my
dog.

I had to do my paper route after school and
I really just wasn't in the mood, which made
me mad for some reason. So I stormed into
the kitchen, fuming, when I saw my dog.
When he saw me his head perked up and his
tail started wagging, so I went over to him
and started petting him. Suddenly, I calmed
down and wanted to do the paper route.

—Camille

Christmas morning, we always go to church. When I was little I always HATED taking an hour away from my precious duty of shredding everything that even remotely resembled a present. I always complained, right up until this past year.

I think it just kinda clicked that this is God's holiday, not mine, so I should at least thank Him by going to 10:00 a.m. Mass.

I believe that God helped me realize this so that I could be a better person.

—Ava Zanatta

I met God in my past when I was at Camp Imadene.

I was signed up for Teen Girls and it was probably one of the best weeks of my life.

We were talking so much about things like self-esteem, boys, bad decisions, and the burdens we kept. It opened my eyes and I learned so much from my cabin leader. I felt as though everything she said was so meaningful.

I saw God in her because of her wisdom and passion to help young girls with their struggles in life; and from this day we still chat on Facebook to keep in touch. She was like the older sister I never had.

—E. Reda

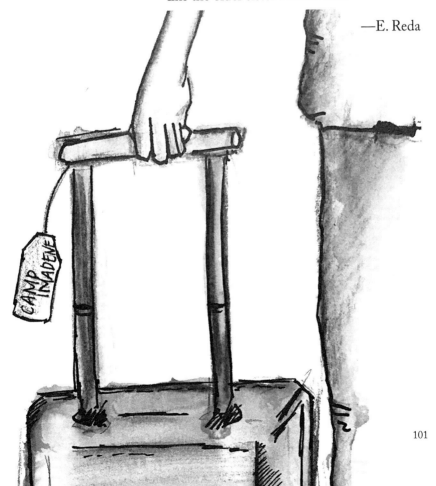

I saw God at the Holocaust Symposium today.

Her name was Lilian and she was a survivor of the Holocaust. When Lilian told us her story, I knew she was talking from her heart. When she talked about the happy times I laughed, and when she spoke of the sad times I cried.

When Lilian talked about her sister's death, I saw something new in Lilian. Suddenly I saw God in her love for her sister and I felt sad for her.

—Maeve P.

One day, maybe one-and-a-half years back, I was walking home from school. Then, all of a sudden, it hit me. I haven't tripped, gotten run over, got shot, been attacked by a swarm of angry bees, been scratched up by a stray cat, been taken down by a large dog, or been bitten by a possum with rabies. There was every chance that these things could have happened, but they didn't.

It was that day that I began to see God
in everything and everybody; every living and nonliving thing.

—Gaurav Sekhon

Today I met God at the end of a long and tiring week of school when I finally heard the bell ring at the end of French class, and then the announcements came on, and then at the end of them I heard, "Goodbye, and have a good weekend."

It was like words from God . . .

—Patrick T.

I met God today in this religion book that I have written. At first I thought of this book as a normal religion assignment. I just thought I would think of something where I found God and then write about it. But now it's not just an assignment.

I'm finding myself thinking about God all the time. I think of something and then figure out how that was God telling me something.

This religion booklet has brought me closer to God. More and more things in my life are related to God now.

—David Boyd

Acknowledgments

The excerpts on pages 5 and 7 are from *The Holy Longing: The Search for a Christian Spirituality,* by Ronald Rolheiser (New York: Doubleday, 1999), pages 95 and 100. Copyright © 1999 by Ronald Rolheiser.

The quote on page 33 is from *Grace in Every Season: Through the Year with Catherine Doherty,* by Mary Achterhoff (Ann Arbor, MI: Servant Publications, 1992), page 22. Copyright © 1992 by Madonna House Publications.

The quote on page 55 is from *God's Enduring Presence: Strength for the Spiritual Journey,* by Joyce Rupp (New London, CT: Twenty-Third Publications, 2008), page 78. Copyright © 2008 by Joyce Rupp.

The quote on page 65 is from *Praying Our Experiences: Twentieth Anniversary Expanded Edition,* by Joseph F. Schmidt, FSC (Winona, MN: Saint Mary's Press, 2000), page 68. Copyright © 2000 by Saint Mary's Press.

During this book's preparation, all citations, facts, figures, names, addresses, telephone numbers, Internet URLs, and other pieces of information cited within were verified for accuracy. The authors and Saint Mary's Press staff have made every attempt to reference current and valid sources, but we cannot guarantee the content of any source, and we are not responsible for any changes that may have occurred since our verification. If you find an error in, or have a question or concern about, any of the information or sources listed within, please contact Saint Mary's Press.